Pusheen the Cat's
Guide to Everything

Also by Claire Belton

I Am Pusheen the Cat

The Many Lives of Pusheen the Cat

Pusheen Coloring Book

Mini Pusheen Coloring Book

Let's Bake!: A Pusheen Cookbook

Pusheen the Cat's
Guide to Everything

Claire Belton

Gallery Books
New York London Toronto Sydney New Delhi

Gallery Books
An Imprint of Simon & Schuster, Inc.
1230 Avenue of the Americas
New York, NY 10020

First Gallery Books trade paperback edition January 2023

GALLERY BOOKS and colophon are registered trademarks of Simon & Schuster, Inc.

For information about special discounts for bulk purchases, please contact Simon & Schuster Special Sales at 1-866-506-1949 or business@simonandschuster.com.

The Simon & Schuster Speakers Bureau can bring authors to your live event. For more information or to book an event, contact the Simon & Schuster Speakers Bureau at 1-866-248-3049 or visit our website at www.simonspeakers.com.

Interior design by Davina Mock-Maniscalco

Manufactured in China

5 7 9 10 8 6 4

Library of Congress Control Number: 2022944844

ISBN 978-1-9821-6541-3
ISBN 978-1-9821-6542-0 (ebook)

For Sarah and Jake

Contents

Pusheen • 1

Stormy • 101

Pip • 119

Sunflower & Biscuit • 135

Sloth • 153

Bo • 171

Cheek • 189

Acknowledgments • 209

Pusheen the Cat's
Guide to Everything

Pusheen

GENDER: Girl

BIRTHDAY: February 18

BEST FEATURE: Big body, small feet

FAVORITE FOOD: All of them

FAVORITE COLOR: Cream

HOBBIES: Being online, snacking, sleeping

ATTRIBUTES: Sweet, curious, lazy

Pusheen's Guide to Fitting In

Plop

Squish

Squash

Ploink

Pusheen's Guide to Crafts

See an idea

Buy supplies

Harder than you thought

See ANOTHER idea

Pudeen

Pusheen's Purrfect Pairings

Cappuccino
+
Cinnamon roll

Macchiato
+
Madeleines

Mocha
+
Macarons

Coffee
+
Donuts

Which One Are You?

Coffee
Full of beans
Dependable

Croisssant
Many layers
A little flaky

Iced mocha
Pretty chill
Sweet

Madeleines
Delicate
Charming

Latte
Easygoing
Creative

Cappuccino
Sophisticated
Romantic

Matcha latte
Energetic
Fluffy

Muffin
Wholesome
Nourishing

Activities to Do with Your Cat

Reading

Puzzles

Gaming

Paranormal investigating

Cat Classes

Geography

Psychology

Physics

History

Pusheen's Guide to Hiding Places

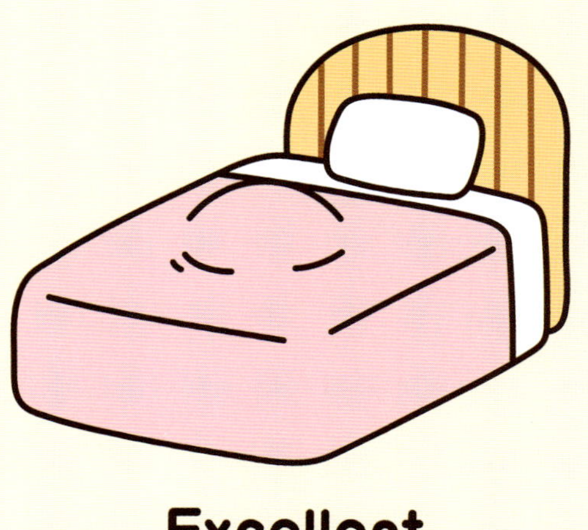

Excellent

Great

Good

Terrible

How to Catch a Leprechaun

Put gold in a pot

Find a rainbow

Catch him!!

Share the wealth

How to Make Your Own Luck

Find a 4-leaf clover

Spot a rainbow

Wish on a star

Get a horseshoe

Irish Mytholosheens

Leprechauneen

Faireen

Selkeen

Bansheen

Cat Sommelier

Unsophisticated, bland

Refreshing, crisp

Notes of fish

Forbidden, sublime

The ~~Dog~~ Cat Days of Summer

Too hot outside

Too hot inside

Too hot to sleep

~~Too hot to eat~~

How to Befriend a Mermaid

1. Follow her siren call

2. Introduce yourself politely

3. Success

How to Eat Ice Cream

On a cone

In a dish

Through a straw

From the source

Pusheen's Guide to Staying Cool

Keep hydrated

Take a cool shower

Find some shade(s)

Be you

Beach Day with Pusheen & Friends

wiches

Building sand~~castles~~

Frizzy

~~Frisbee~~ all day

Throwing

~~Finding~~ shade

Sand

~~Sun~~bathing

Bird

~~People~~ watching

~~Swimming~~

What's Your Road Trip Job?

The navigator

The DJs

The snacker

The napper

The driver

Signs You May Be a Cat Parent

You teach them right from wrong

You keep them entertained

You prepare all of their meals

You love them unconditionally

Home Types for Cats

Fancy Outings (for Your Cat)

Expectation

Reality

Expectation

Reality

Expectation

Reality

Which Dessert Are You?

Ice cream sandwich
Always chilly
Sweet

Éclair
Full of suprises
Fancy

Swiss roll
Diplomat
Unique

Mousse
Elegant
Smooth

Donut
Loves parties
Soft

Dome cake
Dressed to impress
Extra

Cinnamon roll
Early riser
Warm

Tiramisu
Always caffeinated
Multifaceted

Yoga for Cats

Cat pose

Mountain pose

Chair pose

Happy baby pose

Pusheen's TV Guide

Weather forecast

Reality show

True crime

Sci-fi

Pusheenicorn's Guide to Horse Things

Horse blanket

Horse feed

Horse shoes

Pusheen's Guide to Podcasting

Get some gear

Get your audio levels

Get some guests

Forget to hit record

Pusheen's Guide to Baking Substitutions

Honey for sugar

Olive oil for butter

Vinegar for lemon juice

Pans for other pans

Perfect!

How to Make the Perfect Present

Set a budget

Consider their interests

Go shopping

Get creative

Fill with cheer

Present!

Pusheen's Guide to Working from Home

Get up on time

Clear a work space

Minimize distractions

Utilize technology

Pusheen's Guide to Constellations

Big Pipper

Stormius

Sassyopeia

Cat Love Languages

Words of affirmation

Quality time

Acts of service

~~Physical touch~~

A Cat's Guide to the Arts

Painting

Sculpture

Music

Performance art

Pusheen's Gourd Guide

Pumpsheen

Stormy pear

Pipper melon

Butternut sloth

How to Tell If Your Cat Is a Scaredy Cat

Always hiding

Frequently jumpy

Sees ghosts

Good at screaming

#GhostPerks
with Boosheen the Ghost

Infinite snacks

Cold resistant

Maximum privacy

Always delighted

How to Tell If Your Cat Is a *Vampurr*

Sleeps in a box

Has glowing eyes

Has fangs

Likes wet food

Which One Are You?

Kitten
Loves naps
Loves snacks

Puppy
Enjoys walks
There for you

Frog
Kinda jumpy
Questionable taste

Alpaca
Big softie
Loves to frolic

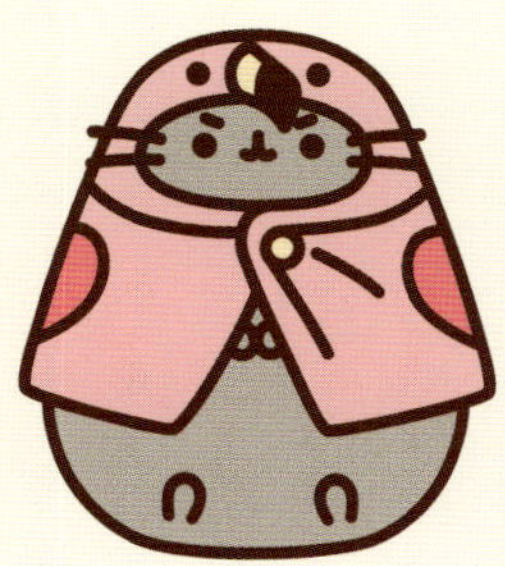

Flamingo
Tall
Excellent dancer

Unicorn
Magical
Good at hiding

Bunny
Good listener
Family oriented

Owl
Wise
Never sleeps

Desk Essentials for Cat People

Ergonomic chair

Wrist rest

Hole puncher

Desk toys

Thanksgiving Roles

The "helper"

The decorator

The observer

The taste tester

How to Define an Ideal Planet

Has great resources

Has a comfortable environment

Has friendly locals

Types of Snowmen

Single scoop

Double-decker

Triple threat

Decuple doom

Winter Fashion (for Your Cat)

Thick fleece

A heavy coat

Fuzzy mittens

Layers

What's Your *Holiday* Style?

Pusheen:

The Classic

Pastel Pusheen:

The Futurist

Dragonsheen:
The Hoard

Mermaidsheen:
The Sunken Treasure

Super Pusheenicorn:
The Dreamscape

Dinosheen:
The Au Naturel

Pusheenicorn's Holiday Tips

Gift your ~~presents~~ presence

Be generous

Light up the room

Slay

How to Plan for Christmas

Wait for it . . .

Wait for it . . .

Celebrate!

Wait for it . . .

New Year's Day Checklist

☑ Get up

☑ Fill up

☑ Clean up

☑ Wrap up

Pusheen's Winter Activities

Sledding

Skiing

Skating

Snuggling

Sweater Weather

Smart

Sporty

Cozy

All natural

Birthday Gift Ideas (for Your Cat)

Something practical

Something fun

Something tasty

Making History with Pusheenosaurus

Survive

Thrive

Leave your mark

...
I look up to remember

I stand in doorways to forget

Stormy

GENDER: Girl

BIRTHDAY: October 24

BEST FEATURE: Very curly

FAVORITE FOOD: Cookies & milk

FAVORITE COLOR: Pink

HOBBIES: Adventuring, grooming herself

ATTRIBUTES: Sweet, reliable, caring

Types of Friends: The Angel

Extremely pure

Very generous

Encourages good behavior

When you spend so much time with your sister you start to dress like her

Stormy's Guide to Getting Ready

Scrub your scruff

Floof your fluff

Polish and buff

Strut your stuff

How to Annoy Your Big Sister

Borrow her things

Get too nosy

Be too cute to get mad at

Uses for Extra Cat Hair

An itchy sweater

A strange wig

A creepy double

Things Stormy Kinda Looks Like

Cotton candy

Sheep

Cloud

Shrub

How to Identify a Middle Child

Wears hand-me-downs

Plays with hand-me-ups

Vies for attention

Surrounded with love

Pusheen's Guide to Having a Little Sister

Play together

Fight together

Scheme together

Bail together

Levels of Fluffiness

Fuzzy

Fluffy

Floofy

Flarfy

Kitten Skills 101

Voice training

Emotional regulation

Hunting

Speed

Pip

GENDER: Boy

BIRTHDAY: June 24

BEST FEATURE: Soft but also pointy

FAVORITE FOOD: Pizza

FAVORITE COLOR: Green

HOBBIES: Annoying his big sisters

ATTRIBUTES: Adventurous, troublemaker

Pip Asks: Can I Eat It?

Maybe

Perhaps

Possibly

NO!!

The Adventures of Pip & Cheek

The adventure

The reality

The adventure

The reality

The adventure

The reality

Pip's Favorite Things

Pip flips

Pip grips

Pip chips

Pip trips

Pip rips

kiss

Pip ~~nips~~

Kitten Adventures

with Pip the Kitten

The adventure

The reality

The adventure

The reality

The adventure

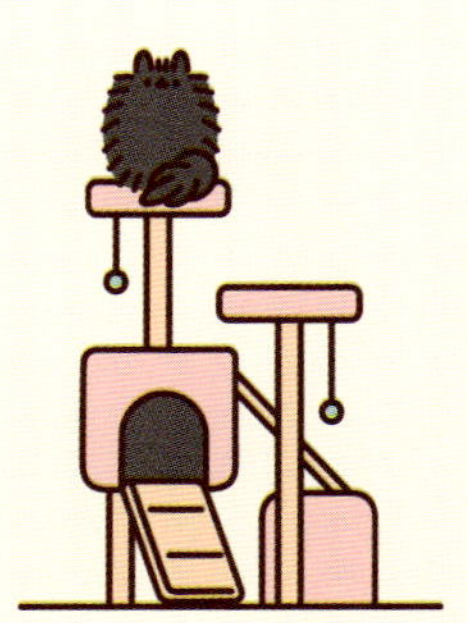

The reality

Movie Night Picks

Pick a movie

Pick a blanket

Pick a snack

Pick a seat

How to Tell If Your Cat Is a Superhero

Can fly

Has secret lair

Fights evil

Has an archnemesis

Pip's Guide to Being an Artist

1. Learn the classics

2. Study from life

3. Explore mediums

4. Make OCs

Pusheen's Guide to Having a Little Brother

Watch him

Adore him

Protect him

Protect yourself

Perks of Being the Baby

Built-in BFFs

Meals made special

Innocent until proven guilty

Sunflower

GENDER: Girl

BIRTHDAY: April 12

BEST FEATURE: Round cheeks

FAVORITE FOOD: Pancakes

FAVORITE COLOR: Yellow

HOBBIES: Being a great mom

ATTRIBUTES: Kind, always there for you

Biscuit

GENDER: Boy

BIRTHDAY: November 10

BEST FEATURE: Elegant mustache

FAVORITE FOOD: Burgers & fries

FAVORITE COLOR: Purple

HOBBIES: Being a great dad

ATTRIBUTES: Kind, good sense of humor

Pusheen Family Tree

Only the Best for Mom

Expectation

Reality

Expectation

Reality

Expectation

Reality

Dad Senses

Sense of smell

Sense of taste

Sense of humor

Common sense

Things You Learn from Mom

Life skills

Good manners

Kindness

Patience

Things You Learn from Dad

How to be well-groomed

How to dress nicely

How to get to work

When to take a break

How
To
Cat

Mother's Day Gift Ideas

Flowers

Breakfast in bed

A beautiful painting

Love

Kitty Parenting Tips

Feed

Sleep

Play

Repeat

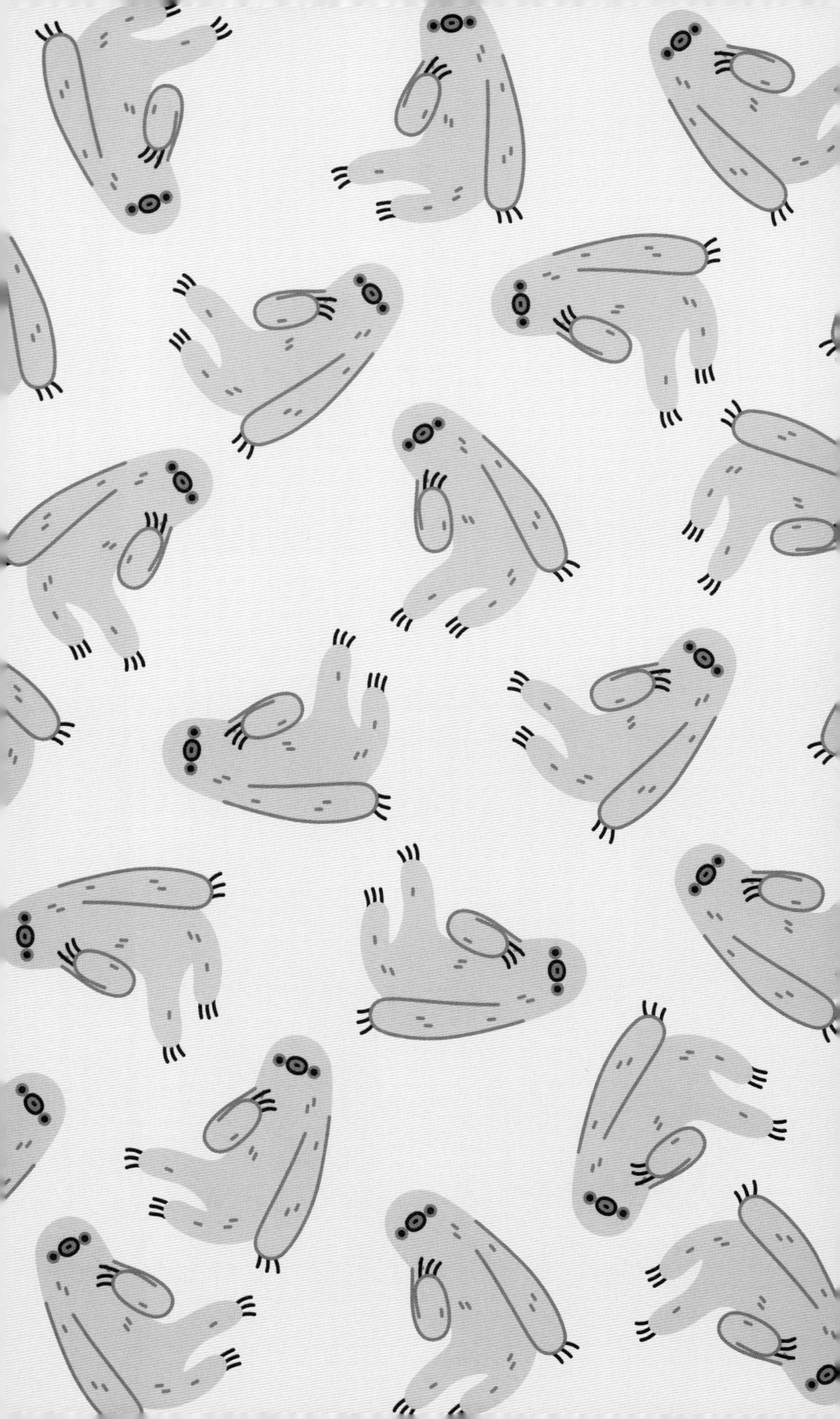

Sloth

GENDER: Boy

BIRTHDAY: August 8

BEST FEATURE: Good looks

FAVORITE FOOD: Salads

FAVORITE COLOR: Green

HOBBIES: Gardening, yoga, being lazy

ATTRIBUTES: Cute, lazy, responsible

Sloth (the sloth)

Good at:
Supporting friends

Really good at:
Being patient

Hobbies:
Staring out windows

Best Feature:
Handsome face

Types of Friends: The Nurturer

Always takes photos

Gifts houseplants

Gives the best hugs

Telling Time with Sloth

Eastern Standard Time

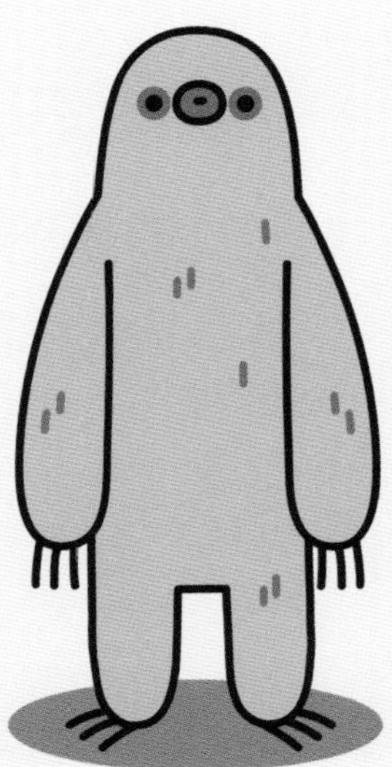

Central Standard Time

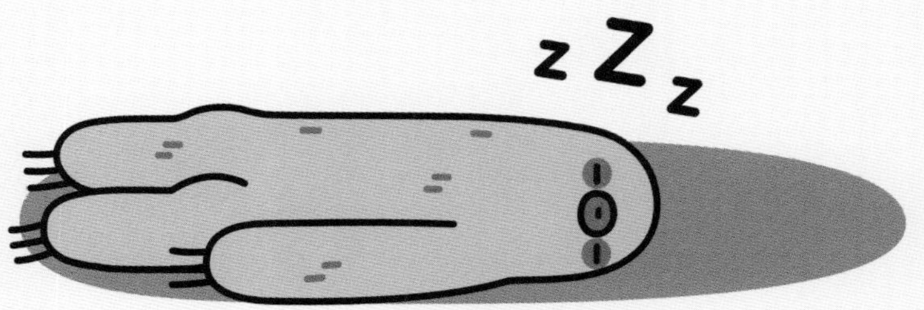

Western Resting Time

Things to Hold On To

A branch

Spare change

Your hat

A good friend

#Slothcare

Enjoy sunshine

Stay hydrated

Spend time in nature

Hug your friends

Things Worth Doing Slowly

Making decisions

Sharing experiences

Creating change

Enjoying life

Sloth's Guide to Being Devastatingly Handsome

Hold yourself well

Have a nice texture

Have some features

Have a good heart

Sloth's Guide to Poses

Seedling pose

Tree pose

Stump pose

Log pose

Sloth's Guide to Being Lazy

Pick things up with your feet

Double up distractions

Text someone in the next room

Order takeout unnecessarily

Bo

GENDER: Girl

BIRTHDAY: March 16

BEST FEATURE: Feet are also hands

FAVORITE FOOD: Fruits with seeds

FAVORITE COLOR: Blue

HOBBIES: Daydreaming, interior design

ATTRIBUTES: Big heart, big dreams

Types of Friends: The Dreamer

Loves to make plans

Always cheers you on

Gives advice they don't take

Bo's Guide to Having a Dinner Party

Plan your menu

Decorate

Set the table

Pour the drinks

Welcome your guests

Bo's Guide to Having a Crush

1. Spot 'em a mile away

2. Make eye contact

3. Confess your feelings

4. Undo undo undo

Types of Parakeet Sounds

SCREEEEEEE

Bo's Summer Fling

• • •

Hi
Read 12:05 PM

How to Deal with Winter

Drink lots of cocoa

Get some good boots

Check the forecast

~~Fly south~~ Improvise

Love Priorities

Love yourself

Love your hobbies

Love what inspires you

Love the ones who love you

Bo-etry

with Bo the Bird

Roses are red

I am blue

You're pretty

Crushcrushcru . . .

Bo's Guide to Falling in Love

1. Think about them

2. Think about them

...

3. Think about them

4. Do nothing

Cheek

GENDER: Boy

BIRTHDAY: May 10

BEST FEATURE: Mysterious rosy cheeks

FAVORITE FOOD: Baked goods

FAVORITE COLOR: Pink & blue

HOBBIES: Baking, playing with Pip

ATTRIBUTES: Tiny but hardworking

How to Make a Cake
with Cheek the Hamster

1. Mix it all

2. Bake it all

3. Frost it all

4. Share it all

Types of Stars

Protostar

Red giant star

Super giant star

You!

Baking for Hamsters

Pepperoni pizza

Chocolate chip cookie

Buttered bread

Blueberry muffin

Things That May or May Not Be in Cheek's Cheeks

Types of Friends: The Foodie

Knows the best spots

Bakes for everyone

Always has room

4 Ways to Show You Care

1. Prep for them

2. Cook for them

3. Bake for them

4. Feed them

Advantages to Being Tiny

Big snacks

Big screens

Big naps

Big hugs

Daily Hamster Essentials

Clean bedding

A hamster ball

A water bottle

Snacks

Cheek's Adventures

Expectation

Reality

Expectation

Reality

Expectation

Reality

zZ
Naptime

Pusheen's Guide to Happiness

Practice gratitude

Eat well

Get plenty of sleep

Surround yourself with
the ones you love

Acknowledgments

I would like to extend my sincere thanks to all the people who helped to bring this book to life.

Thanks first and foremost to our creative director, Katie Belton, and the whole of our creative team for all of their hard work and contributions to this book and all things Pusheen!

Thanks as always to our director of project management, Cassandra Lipin, and director of licensing, Cate D'Allessandro, whose combined organization and coordination skills are invaluable on large projects such as this book.

Thank you as well to our fantastic managing director, Mary Hennessy, for all her help running Pusheen Corp., and to my partner and Pusheen cofounder, Andrew Duff, for all that he does to support me. Their combined efforts allow me to spend more and more of my time drawing and creating!

Another huge thank-you to my ever supportive and enthusiastic book crew, literary agent Myrsini Stephanides, editors Lauren Spiegel and Rebecca Strobel, and the rest of the team at Simon & Schuster who helped to make this wonderful book!

And last but not least, thank YOU for reading it and for supporting Pusheen!

For More Pusheen, Find Her Online

www.Pusheen.com

Instagram: @Pusheen

Twitter: @Pusheen

TikTok: @Pusheen

Facebook: @Pusheen

YouTube: @PusheentheCat

About the Author

Claire Belton is an artist and entrepreneur based in Chicago. She spends her time petting cats, drawing cats, and pursuing cat-related endeavors.

About Pusheen

Pusheen is a tubby tabby cat who brings smiles and laughter to people all around the world. She became famous through her animated comics and GIFs posted on Pusheen.com, as well as through her widely used animated stickers on Facebook, Instagram, iMessage, and other platforms.